DISCIPLING DISCIPLINE

in the

CHRISTIAN SCHOOL

by

Rev. Paul V. Bickel

Discipling Discipline in the Christian School
by Rev. Paul V. Bickel

Printed in the United States of America

ISBN 9781615790883

Unless otherwise indicated, Bible quotations are taken from the English Standard Version of the Bible. Copyright © 2001 by Crossway Bibles, a division of Good News Publishers: Concordia Edition, printed in the United States of America, published by Concordia Publishing House, St. Louis, MO 63118.

www.xulonpress.com

Dedicated to my father, Victor F. Bickel— next to Jesus, the biggest influence in my faith and understanding of education.

$\Longrightarrow$

A cknowledgement and appreciation for help in the completion of this book go to:

My wife Martha for editing and contributing to the final draft of this book;

My son Lukas and daughter Rachel Herlein for reading and advising me on the content of this book;

Dr. Russ Moulds for evaluating, contributing to the content, and encouraging me to complete the book. His dedication to Christian education compelled him to give much time and attention to this project for the purpose of helping fellow teachers.

Table of Contents

INTRODUCTION

I have been involved in Christian education for over fifty-five years, first as a student and then as a teacher. The most effective teachers I have had and observed exhibited some common traits that I believe to be essential in this unique Spiritual calling. This study is an attempt to relate those characteristics and procedures to others in the teaching ministry who are looking for ways to be more intentional about having an eternal impact on their students. My goal is to help Christian teachers find ways to fulfill their compelling desire to reach souls with the gospel of Jesus Christ.

Discipling discipline is built on the following foundation: Love God, Obey Scripture, Build Community, Love Yourself, Respect Yourself, Love Students, Respect Students. *Discipling* discipline seeks to use disciplinary situations as opportunities to create *disciples* for Jesus who live for Him in all facets of their lives. The objective of *Discipling* discipline is not simply to stop undesirable behavior but to help students develop a way of life that is guided by the Spirit and a blessing to God's kingdom.

That is not to say that the methods and ideas presented here are the best or only way to *disciple* and discipline in the Christian classroom. Most methods of discipline work when they are done in genuine Christian love, but my concern is that many do not incorporate a *discipling* element. I am confident that you will find useful concepts and insights to consider even if you do not choose to follow all of the material presented here.

I have seen, for young teachers especially, that classroom discipline can be their undoing; and for veteran teachers, discipline has often become routine and has lost its Spiritual effectiveness. Because there are so many secular approaches to this aspect of education, I felt compelled to add this approach to discipline to the mix. Christian teachers can then contemplate and use whatever they find helpful.

As we face the challenge of teaching in the post-modern era, it is crucial that, like generations before us, we use practices that are based on God's timeless Word. Throughout history, Christians have had to overcome the cultural pressure to move away from God and to use a secular approach to life. Francis Schaeffer's *How Then Should We Live?* (also available in a video series) is a great resource that helps us understand how these world influences have changed us as a people. We don't know what new approach to life is next or what label it will be given, but we know it will come. The only real defense against these earthly philosophies is to follow the truth of scripture.

I believe this study to be foundationally based in scripture and Spiritually guided using Jesus, the Master Teacher, as the perfect example. This presentation is not based on rigorous research or an in-depth study of discipline in education. I am a practitioner, not a theorist. I am not an eloquent writer and without my wife Martha's help, you would have a hard time reading this. I like what Luther said: "Truth is mightier than eloquence, Spirit greater than genius, faith more than education." I therefore offer a scripture-based, Spiritually motivated application of God's Word to an important facet of our sacred calling.

I've been in the "trenches," and this document comes from a desire to help and support fellow soldiers of the cross in the most important quest on earth, the salvation of souls. Christian teachers have a unique and privileged opportunity seldom afforded other believers. Parents entrust their most treasured gift from God, their child, to our care. God entrusts to us the imparting of the most precious gift He has to offer, salvation in Jesus. We, as His servants, have a solemn obligation to do the absolute best we can—to be as effective in our calling as possible.

I am hopeful that this document will meet multiple needs. I see it as being useful for private or school-wide Bible study. It could be the basis for looking at discipline policies of an individual classroom or an entire school system. It could be used for faculty devotions or pre or post school meetings. I have purposely not given answers to the questions posed at the end of each chapter. I believe that would be disrespectful to you and to God as well. I trust the Holy Spirit's power through the Word to lead you to God-pleasing answers that are beneficial to you and your Christian school. This is not about my convincing you to think as I do, but rather, it is an opportunity to allow the Spirit to guide us all to be the most effective teachers we can be in the *discipling* process to which we have given our lives. I pray that however this handbook is used, it gives all glory to God, and that through it He blesses all of our ministries.

God's Word on the Subject: II Corinthians 10:3ff, I Corinthians 1:18ff

CHAPTER 1

DISCIPLE CHRISTIANS

A s you read this study, it will be helpful to be aware of some assumptions I have made and what I mean when I use the terms "Christian" and "D*iscipl*e." (I have italicized the word "*disciple*" in order to distinguish it from the word "discipline." As I was reading, my dyslexia kept getting the two words mixed up, and I found it easier this way. It also emphasizes the importance of the objective of our teaching.)

Let's begin with some basics. Scripture teaches that for Christians the number one objective in life is to give glory to God, their creator. Christians believe the Bible to be the only rule and norm for life that shows them how to live to God's glory. All humans are sinners and are in need of a savior, *and* Jesus Christ of the Bible is that savior. Faith, given to us by the Holy Spirit, is the tool by which we take hold of the forgiveness won for us by Jesus. Good works are done in response to *being* saved, not done in order to *be* saved. All Christians have the same purpose in life: to share the good news of salvation in Jesus with everyone near and far. It gives God the greatest glory when others see, as we do, how He worked out our salvation at the cost of the blood of Jesus on the cross.

Christians are, therefore, in the ongoing process of evangelizing and then *discipling* anyone and everyone. They invoke the Holy Spirit through His sacred Word so people can walk with the rest of

Christendom in faith toward God. True believers help each other in the task of living the sanctified life by *discipling* each other. We do not get through life alone. God has given us the body of Christ, the Church, to support and sustain us in our journey to heaven. *Discipling* is the activity that encourages and motivates fellow Christians to endure to the end. You have chosen the profession of Christian teaching to fulfill your calling and carry out your mission and ministry in a more direct way than most Christians have the privilege of doing. As a *disciple* of Jesus, you have a desire to be as effective as you possibly can be in *discipling* your students.

As educators, we have been conditioned to set objectives in our lesson planning and to work to these ends. The objective of Christian education is the development of *disciples. Disciples,* according to scripture, are those who trust Jesus for the forgiveness of their sins (justification) and desire to live their lives for Him (sanctification) in response to His love. "So Jesus said to the Jews who had believed in him, 'If you abide in my word, you are truly my disciples, and you will know the truth, and the truth will set you free'" (John 8:31-32). He also told those who believed in Him that if they wanted to come after Him, they must take up their crosses and follow Him. "And whoever does not take his cross and follow me is not worthy of me" (Matt.10:38). He invited His *disciples* to become fishers of men. "And Jesus said to them, 'Follow me, and I will make you fishers of men'" (Mark 1:17). He prayed that His *disciples* be one with Him as He and His Father are one. "Holy Father, keep them in your name, which you have given me, that they may be one, even as we are one. I do not ask for these only, but also for those who will believe in me through their word, [21] that they may all be one, just as you, Father, are in me, and I in you, that they also may be in us, so that the world may believe that you have sent me. The glory that you have given me I have given to them, that they may be one even as we are one" (John 17: 11, 20-22).

Our objective, then, is to train our students in Jesus' word of truth—to set them free from their sin and free to serve Him. Our desire is to send out a mighty force for Jesus—people who love being a part of the body of Christ, who feel and know the presence of God and are at one with Him, who know how to forgive, who understand and can use scripture, who have learned to reject the way of the world, who can be in the world but not of it, who recognize Satan wherever and whenever he is active, who are ready in season and out of season to share His Word, who are compelled by His love to speak out for Him, and who are willing to be ridiculed for their faith—in other words, to send out a mighty force of those who have developed a Christ centered way of life. They will joyfully give themselves to Him "in whom they live and move and have their being" (Acts 17:28). Led by the Holy Spirit, they will serve God in all things.

In some ways, I envy the training of some religious groups like the orthodox Jews or the Amish. Even though I disagree with their doctrine, I can see that they are much more successful than we are in committing the next generation to a way of life. I realize that this is often achieved by using legalistic practices, but for those who buy into it, there is no separation between who they are, what they believe and how they live. Too often we teach a detached, ritualized religion that is separated from the reality of our daily lives. Too often we tack on religion as another club we belong to.

We teach facts and information from the Bible but are not successful in getting the students to see the Word's connection to their personal lives; or we get them so pumped up on certain notions about the Holy Spirit that they lose touch with reality and are no "earthly" good. Jesus' *disciples* were real people who lived real lives and yet lived and breathed for Him. They didn't always have their theology right, but they were committed to Him. They allowed the Holy Spirit to lead them in their daily lives. You could no more separate their love for Jesus from their thinking and doing than you could separate heat from fire.

We, as Christian educators, should especially show how faith is central to every aspect of life. This is how *discipling* happens. When students see how we apply faith and God's Word to all situations the community encounters, they begin to understand what being a *disciple* of Jesus means. This study is an attempt to more closely connect our faith to the daily lives of everyone in the Christian school environment. Chapel services, religion classes, Bible studies, and other organized methods are important, but they are scheduled and formalized. The students and parents *expect* spirituality in these situations. Therefore these organized methods are not as effective in establishing a way of life as are spontaneous events. The application of faith and spirituality to day to day unplanned situations in the school is where the student can be most effectively *discipled*. This is why I believe it is in discipline that we make the biggest impact on our students.

QUESTIONS FOR FURTHER DISCUSSION:

1. What percentage of your graduates would you judge are *disciples* as described above?

_____

2. What area of your school's overall approach produces the largest number of *disciples*?

_____

_____

_____

3. What non-structured situations could you use to *disciple* your students?

_____

_____

_____

4. What area of your life is not as *disciple* focused as you would like?

_____

_____

_____

5. What is the difference between piety and *discipleship*?

_____

_____

_____

6. What is the difference between religion and faith?

_____

_____

_____

7. What school policies lead to *discipleship*?

_____

_____

_____

8. What school policies hinder *discipleship*?

_____

_____

_____

9. Describe the gap between the behavior you teach and want as guided by Scripture and how your students and staff actually live.

_____

_____

_____

10. How would the implementation of this passage look in the classroom? "If anyone comes to me and does not hate his own father and mother and wife and children and brothers and sisters, yes, and even his own life, he cannot be my disciple. 33 So therefore, any one of you who does not renounce all that he has cannot be my disciple" (Luke 14:26).

_____

_____

_____

11. What is the fruit of *discipleship* in this passage? "By this my Father is glorified, that you bear much fruit and so prove to be my disciples" (John 15:8).

_____

_____

_____

12. What joy have you experienced as you have watched students grow as described in this verse? "And we all, with unveiled face, beholding the glory of the Lord, are being transformed into the same image from one degree of glory to another. For this comes from the Lord who is the Spirit" (II Cor. 3:18).

_____

_____

_____

More of God's Word on the Subject: John 6:28-29, I Timothy 2:3-4, II Timothy 2:2, Matthew 24:13, Ephesians 4:1, Luke 16:1-15, II Corinthians 2:12-17, I John 3:1-3, Matthew 7:21-23

CHAPTER 2

TEACH AND DISCIPLINE

The reason I have chosen a thesis on discipline in an attempt to improve Christian teaching in general, is that discipline is where teachers ultimately win over or lose their students. It is through disciplinary encounters that the students decide if teachers are going to help them and be on their side or not. It is in disciplinary confrontations that they will decide if a teacher can be trusted and cares about them as people or not. This is also true in the case of administrators. During an act of discipline is about the only time most students have contact with administrators. These are the encounters, then, on which the students base their evaluation of principals and those in authority other than teachers.

It is our disciplinary actions that reveal who we really are. The students will see either the love of God coming from a committed Christian or the self preservation of a self-serving person in authority. For most students it is that black and white. Consequently, how we discipline affects our ability to *disciple* our students for Jesus. It makes or breaks the ministry we are trying to carry out.

I was a new teacher at Baltimore Lutheran High School. Chris walked into my third period of the first day of classes. He sat down in a chair separate from all the others, facing the wrong direction. He had a ball cap pulled down to his eyebrows. When he began yelling across the room at his apparent buddies, I guessed he had decided to take on the task of testing the new teacher. I had many options to choose from as to how to handle Chris. My goal is that after working through this study, you will know what I did and why it worked. I found out later that many of the other teachers had, for the most part, written Chris off as a lost cause. By the way, after he graduated he stopped in from time to time just to talk with me about life.

If we are unsuccessful in our ability to discipline, students will turn us off, and nothing we say will matter to them. Oh, we might get them to sit still and not disrupt "our" class or to even take notes and pass "our" tests, but we will not have *discipled* them. This is what should make our classroom different than the public school classroom down the street. We have an added agenda of affecting their Spiritual lives and leading them closer to Jesus. If we have turned them off by our discipline, we can't *disciple*.

Your academic subjects are important, but few students evaluate you on your grasp of the scholastic material. First and foremost, they want to know what kind of person you are. In a list of qualities students want in their teachers "they like me" ranks high along with "fair" and "is real." These characteristics emerge from our discipline, not our math, literature or history classes. This is also true for administrators and their relationship with students and their parents. Students and their parents are more concerned with how you treat them than whether you have a good teacher's handbook or not. To use an old adage: They don't care how much you know until they know how much you care."

Through our discipline they will or will not see Jesus. As we examine His life, we realize that His ministry revolved around relationships, not accomplishments. He used His miracles to draw people into relationship and to demonstrate His connection with His Father. His parables explained the personal connection between God and humankind. His judgments of the unfaithful were to create accountability for the sinners and draw them into relationship with a forgiving God. Most of His discourses had a distinct disciplinary (not punitive) element, and yet His love for them was unmistakably there. Our teaching should look the same.

Therefore it is in relationships that we will have the best chance to be Christ-like. My hypothesis is that in *disciplining*, we will have the most frequent opportunities to develop relationships in the classroom.

Our subject matter has a different impact on students because of our role as evaluators. In other words, we have an obligation to give grades for their work. This is the part of our work that they expect. It has potential for relationship building, but it is not nearly as strong and intense as when we discipline.

There are, of course, other situations that avail us of relationship building, such as coaching, directing dramas or choir, or sponsoring a club. But these activities also involve discipline. Establishing relationships with students in informal ways almost as friends is possible, but that will only be with a handful of students whose personalities click with yours. I am not discouraging those connections as long as they maintain a clear distinction between the teacher- pupil roles. But most of your students won't get to know the real you that way. They will have to wait until they see you in action in the classroom, day after day, under all kinds of circumstances, the most telling of which will be your method of discipline.

All students at a very early age have learned that adults have two sides to them, one when the students are behaving and one when they are misbehaving. They will hold final judgment of what kind of teacher you are until they see how you function in both situations. All the warm caring instruction can be undone in one botched disciplinary action, but you can botch lesson after lesson and they will still love you if your discipline is God-like in nature. If you carry out your discipline as a spiritual tool, you can *disciple* so much more effectively because the students will be with you and not against you. An added benefit is that they are more willing to listen to your scholastic material as well. I believe this is one of the reasons why Christian schools are Spiritually *and* academically successful.

Another basic concept of this process is that teaching is *discipling* and *discipling* is teaching. It is not accidental that Jesus' followers were called "*disciples*" and He was called "Teacher." Whenever Christians are active in the educational process, *discipling* and teaching are intrinsically woven together. Throughout history people who followed a leader or philosopher were called *disciples*. I had a seminary professor who had his own *disciples*. There was even a special name for this group of seminarians. I am sure this professor did not intend to establish such a group, it just happened. What he did intend was to open students' eyes to the truth of God's Word. Because he was so intense and committed to his students and to his Savior, many often sat at his feet to learn as much as possible. He could even "hold class" in the cafeteria or in the library. All Christians are called to turn others to Jesus and help them become His *disciples*, but this is especially true of Christian educators.

Jesus won people over by His teachings *and* His love. They accepted His teachings because He loved them and He taught the truth. He also was not afraid to discipline. His was not the sentimental weak kind of love that is so prevalent today. He often showed his love in hard, unyielding disciplinary actions and words. His confrontational approach to sinners was an integral part of His total ministry. His objective never changed. No matter what He was talking about, He was developing *disciples* that would follow Him into heaven. It was always about them and for them.

I am convinced that unless we *disciple* students, we don't really get to teach. Even in secular settings, speakers know that unless they get their audience on their side, nothing will be accomplished. Sales people are great at this. They know that unless they win you over—*disciple* you—their chances of selling their product are pretty slim. I am not advocating a pushy salesman approach to teaching, but we do need to be *discipling*, winning students over for Jesus. In the public school system they are doing the same, only they *disciple* for different reasons and purposes. Our *discipling* is for the Lord and has eternal consequences.

Conversely, if we don't teach, we don't *disciple*. I am not talking about math and science. If we are not teaching life as Jesus did, we are missing our calling, and our ministry is an empty exercise of secular instruction. Situations that demand discipline are optimum *discipling* moments that should not be displaced by using simple control tactics or punishment. Great discussions about life's choices and purpose come out of Jesus' style of discipline. Isn't this why most of us chose Christian teaching in the first place? We answered His call to share our faith in Jesus so others would know the joy and peace we have in Him. That is *discipling*.

QUESTIONS FOR FURTHER DISCUSSION:

1. How can we maintain the professional status of teacher and still get Spiritually close to our students?

_____

_____

_____

2. Describe the best Christian teacher you have ever had and list his/her characteristics.

_____

_____

_____

3. Describe the unique relationship Jesus had with his *disciples*.

_____

_____

_____

4. Describe a disciplinary situation that affected your relationship with your students. Did it weaken or strengthen your ability to witness to them?

_____

_____

_____

5. What gives students the right to judge their teachers?

_____

_____

_____

6. What is the difference between discipline and punishment?

_____

_____

_____

7. How does motivation change outcome as a teacher or administrator deals with student discipline?

_____

_____

_____

8. What does painful mean in this quote from Hebrews 12?
"And have you forgotten the exhortation that addresses you as sons?
    "My son, do not regard lightly the discipline of the Lord,
        nor be weary when reproved by him.
    [6] For the Lord disciplines the one he loves,
        and chastises every son whom he receives."
[7] It is for discipline that you have to endure. God is treating you as sons. For what son is there whom his father does not discipline? [8] If you are left without discipline, in which all have participated, then you are illegitimate children and not sons. [9] Besides this, we have had earthly fathers who disciplined us and we respected them. Shall we not much more be subject to the Father of spirits and live? [10] For they disciplined us for a short time as it seemed best to them, but he disciplines us for our good, that we may share his holiness. [11] For the moment all discipline seems painful rather than pleasant, but later it yields the peaceful fruit of righteousness to those who have been trained by it" (Heb. 12:5-11).

_____

_____

_____

9. How should you discipline if you are God's instrument as a disciplinarian?

_____

_____

_____

10. Share a time when the promise given here was fulfilled in your personal life or your teaching.
"For the moment all discipline seems painful rather than pleasant, but later it yields the peaceful fruit of righteousness to those who have been trained by it." (Hebrews 12:11)

_____

_____

_____

More of God's Word on the Subject: I Corinthians 9:19ff, Ephesians 4:1-16, Mark 10:17ff, Luke 9:51-55, Luke 22:24-27

CHAPTER 3

LOVE GOD

I almost omitted this next topic in the discussion because I thought it was self-understood when addressing "Christian" teachers. I realize now that I was being naive. Even committed Christians lose focus from time to time. We all need to re-evaluate our relationship with God regularly. In fact, this re-evaluation is the most important of the building blocks upon which to establish a method of discipline.

The importance of this step is abundantly clear in the story of Peter's reinstatement as Jesus' *disciple*. Three times Jesus asks Peter if he loves Jesus. Three times Peter assures Jesus that he does love Him. Jesus' response is, "Feed My sheep" (John 21:15-19). I think it is a fair assumption, then, that loving Him is a prerequisite to being about the task of feeding His sheep or, in light our discussion here, a prerequisite to Christian education and *discipling*. Loving Jesus motivates us to take the focus off ourselves and place it squarely on Him.

Christian schools too often give this building block lip service. The faculty meetings and the time spent trying to be more "successful" are focused on the business of the day. Consequently, our Spirituality consists of quick "schmaltzy" pre-canned devotions so we can move on to the more *important* things. I pray this does not describe your school. I thankfully worked under a principal who did take Spirituality seriously. He made sure we spent the first half of our faculty meetings in Bible study and growing in faith. We prayed together and encouraged one another in our shared ministry. It was the tightest and most effective faculty on which I have ever served.

I am convinced that most burnout among Christian teachers results from the loss of connection to Jesus as the purpose for their teaching. The joy we experience in this task of Christian education is in direct proportion to the degree to which we offer ourselves to Him in love.

A truth that has become increasingly apparent to me is that everything *is* about Jesus. The Old Testament was written to reveal Jesus. In fact, one of the fun things to do in teaching the Old Testament is to find Jesus in every account and character. I was frustrated when my children came home from Sunday school with some moral lesson they had learned from an Old Testament story, while no mention was made of Jesus. The whole purpose of the Spirit's revelation is Jesus. It is through Jesus that we see God and His love. Jesus is the head of the body, the Church. God's promise is that we will reign with Jesus in heaven. The whole purpose of our existence is to bring others to faith in Jesus.

No matter what vocation we choose, our God-given calling is saving souls in Jesus through the power of the Holy Spirit. Humans are the only things that will be going to heaven from this earth. The body, soul, and spirit of every person on Earth are worth our greatest effort. If we love Jesus and saving souls is what matters to Him, then it naturally matters to us.

This is how we demonstrate our love for God and keep the first commandment, "Have no other gods before Me." It is not an accident that the first commandment is the *first* commandment. This commandment is first, not because He needs anything from us or He is self-centered, but it is because every good flows from this relationship. God only gives us commandments that result in blessings. This, the first of all the commandments, offers us the greatest blessings.

I once asked in class at the seminary if God's laws had a practical purpose as well as a Spiritual one. The professor was adamant that they only had Spiritual significance. I disagreed with him then, and I have not been convinced otherwise since. God is love, and His laws are based in love. They do have eternal Spiritual relevance, of course, but they also demonstrate His love in that through obedience we are blessed with an abundant life here on earth. For example, He gave rules about washing to protect His people from germs. It reminds us of being washed clean in the blood of Christ, but it also protected the Jews from infections and diseases, the causes of which were unknown to mankind at that time.

He is our loving Father who has made an incredible commitment to each one of us through His Son and the Holy Spirit. When we offer ourselves as instruments in His kingdom, we are opening ourselves up to an intimate relationship with Him that is unique and humbling. How He uses us, the broken vessels we are, is a miracle in itself. May you find true peace and joy in serving Him in love as His servants.

QUESTIONS FOR FURTHER DISCUSSION:

1. List ten things that a stranger to your campus would notice that would make them aware that you, as an institution, serve our triune God.

_____

_____

_____

2. Do the same for individual classrooms.

_____

_____

_____

3. What are the Spiritual prerequisites for a faculty or staff person to serve at your Christian school?

_____

_____

_____

4. What are your personal barriers that are keeping you from loving God as fully as you would like?

_____

_____

_____

5. What are the policies or attitudes of your school community that may be hindering putting God first and foremost in the daily lives of students and staff?

_____

_____

_____

6. Evaluate the influence you are having on your students in regard to their love for God.

_____

_____

_____

7. What opportunities do you have to talk openly and personally about your love for God to your fellow ministers?

_____

_____

_____

8. What motivates you to obey this instruction? "And now, Israel, what does the Lord your God require of you, but to fear the Lord your God, to walk in all his ways, to love him, to serve the Lord your God with all your heart and with all your soul" (Deut. 10:12).

_____

_____

_____

9. How do we *believe* the love God has for us? "So we have come to know and to believe the love that God has for us. God is love, and whoever abides in love abides in God, and God abides in him" (I John 4:16).

_____

_____

_____

More of God's Word on the Subject: Luke 7:47, Matthew 9:35-38, James 1:17, Ephesians 1:10, I Corinthians 3:21-23

CHAPTER 4

LOVE YOURSELF

I pray that I have convinced you that *discipleship* is what we are about, and that discipline is a crucial tool available to teachers who wish to draw students closer to God. If so, then consider the next subject in being a successful *discipler*. From a right relationship with God through the Holy Spirit comes a right relationship with yourself. Loving yourself is another block in the foundation on which to build an effective disciplinary system.

If we as individuals bring all kinds of unfinished business and unresolved baggage to the classroom, we jeopardize the effectiveness of our time with the students. It is true in all aspects of our lives. Work, play, marriage, and family are all affected by our view of ourselves. There has to be a total acceptance of who we are just for who we are. If Jesus' forgiveness is not truly lived out minute by minute, we become vulnerable to fears and doubts, and our insecurities will come out sideways in dealing with our students. We all have scars from our past, and it takes a lot of hard, painful work to understand them and not have them influence us; but it can and must be done if we are not going to adversely impact our students.

After counseling countless church members, I came to realize that we all have issues to deal with. The only people who don't have issues are those who *only* knew people who were *always* loving and supportive and *only* did things as Christ would do them *all the time.* Do you get the point? No such person exists. The degree to which you have been wounded and the extent to which this is still affecting you depends on how it was handled when the negative events took place, how severe they were and how frequently they occurred. Children, for the most part, are forced to swallow their pain and move on. That is why many people wait to address their pain until they are adults and are powerful enough to attack some of these problems. I have found that many never deal with their pain, and the unresolved issues gain a power of their own, stealing joy from people's lives.

By far the most hurtful situations involve divorce, alcoholism, abuse of any kind (sexual, physical, emotional or verbal), and abandonment. In my experience, abandonment is the worst of all. It can be the result of parents who were workaholics or who were emotionally unavailable through mental illness or neglect. Perhaps it is the result of the child being put up for adoption. Even if the dysfunction started in a previous generation, it can still have a surprising strength in affecting present day life because the patterns and consequences will be passed on from generation to generation.

Consider this passage from Exodus: "The Lord passed before him and proclaimed, 'The Lord, the Lord, a God merciful and gracious, slow to anger, and abounding in steadfast love and faithfulness, [7] keeping steadfast love for thousands, forgiving iniquity and transgression and sin, but who will by no means clear the guilty, visiting the iniquity of the fathers on the children and the children's children, to the third and the fourth generation'" (Exodus 34:6-7). God forgives the repentant sinner, but the natural earthly consequences of sin are not instantly removed. The consequences are mitigated through living the sanctified life in obedience to His Word. This is the hard work to which I am referring.

If you experienced any of these hurtful situations as a child and have not dealt with them in any meaningful way, you will lose, to a lesser or greater degree, your effectiveness as a disciplinarian. You will have discipline, but it will not be *discipling* in nature. It may, in fact, manifest itself as punishment rather than *discipling.* I do not believe in living in the past or using it as an excuse for not moving forward in life. I *do* believe in gaining an understanding of ourselves so Satan can't use our wounds as tools to weaken our ministry. This is where many of our bad motives come from which will be dealt with in a later topic. Being thoroughly honest with ourselves is absolutely essential here. Please don't brush off the significance of your negative experiences as they have certainly fashioned you in the same way that positive experiences have given you the good you have to offer.

Of course, the most important and freeing step is to embrace the total forgiveness Jesus offers us on the cross and to believe that Jesus truly does love you. If God in all of His holiness can love me - the sinner that I am - who am I to say I am unlovable? It is disrespectful to God to not love yourself. Jesus died for you. The weakness we bring to the classroom so often comes from a fear that we will not be accepted. God's love should drive that from us so that we can stand before our students without any *need* to be accepted by anyone. In Jesus we are whole and complete.

If you don't like you, who will? If you enter the classroom with an overriding sense of shame, guilt, insecurity or doubt, the children will see it immediately. I am not talking about a cocky bravado or oversized ego, but rather a sincere sense of well-being that warmly embraces who you are. If we want to be effective teachers and disciplinarians and *disciplers*, then this is a constant goal for which we must strive. It is a never ending battle, and Satan will not leave it alone; therefore, it takes perpetual care.

One of the great tools we have in developing a good self image and a good litmus test of where we are in this battle is good "self talk." Take note of the way you talk to yourself. Is it berating or uplifting? Are your adjectives negative or positive? Do you rehearse failures more than successes? Do you confess your sins and learn from them, or do you beat yourself up with them?

Looking into the compassionate, accepting face of Jesus on a regular basis is also helpful in the quest of acceptance of one's self. The private study of His Word and a fervent prayer life bring us into His presence like nothing else can. He is also visible in the face of fellow Christians who have learned to love themselves by being loved by Jesus. Your brothers and sisters in Christ will see your gifts and devotion to God and help you to develop the self esteem God wants you to have. This is why a close connection to a loving church family is so essential to our ministry. Worshiping Him often and receiving His body and blood are critical to the life of serving Him and *discipling* His children in a healthy self-loving way.

QUESTIONS FOR FURTHER DISCUSSION:

1. What events or people in your life have made it hard for you to love yourself?

_____

_____

_____

2. How does this verse help justify loving yourself? "And a second is like it: You shall love your neighbor as yourself" (Matt. 22:39).

_____

_____

_____

3. List five ways you can develop a deeper love and appreciation for yourself?

_____

_____

_____

4. What are some ways you can help your students love themselves?

_____

_____

_____

5. How do your colleagues encourage each other to love themselves?

_____

_____

_____

6. What does loving oneself look like?

_____

_____

_____

7. How does loving yourself differ from being self-centered?

_____

_____

_____

8. How does your relationship with Jesus help you love yourself?

_____

_____

_____

9. How does loving yourself give love to God? "In the same way husbands should love their wives as their own bodies. He who loves his wife loves himself. [29] For no one ever hated his own flesh, but nourishes and cherishes it, just as Christ does the church, [30] because we are members of his body" (Eph. 5:28-30).

_____

_____

_____

10. How does loving yourself show love to your fellow believers?

_____

_____

_____

11. How does this passage help you feel good about yourself? "No longer do I call you servants, for the servant does not know what his master is doing; but I have called you friends, for all that I have heard from my Father I have made known to you" (John 15:15).

_____

_____

_____

More of God's Word on the Subject: Romans 6, I John 3:1-3, Exodus 20:5, Exodus 34:6-7, I Timothy 1:5, Philippians 4:10

CHAPTER 5

RESPECT YOURSELF

Adding this next block to the foundation of effective *discipling* is made much easier if we do love God and ourselves as discussed before. You may wonder how respecting yourself is different from loving yourself. To me, love is personal and private, whereas respect is less personal, more public and professionally based. Our degree of professionalism is pivotal in how we will come across to our students.

Do you enter the classroom knowing that you are going to be successful? Do you covey an air of confidence that says you know what you are doing? Are you the adult in the room who will successfully carry out the teacher role for them? In order to say yes to these types of questions, teachers need to be prepared. They need to have their lessons thoroughly worked out. There is no substitute for well thought out lesson plans in keeping order in a classroom.

I do not intend to put teachers under the pressure of having to know everything there is to know in their discipline or to have all the answers. On the contrary, respect for yourself is demonstrated when you respond to a question you don't have the answer for with a confident assurance that you will find the answer as soon as possible. Of course, you must follow up with the promised answer. Better yet, research the answer together with the students and demonstrate a thirst for knowledge.

Students see right through a lack of respect teachers may have for themselves. As a principal watching teachers and observing student teachers, I have often seen a reluctance to expect the standards of respect their role deserves. Students talk while the teacher is talking, or they get up to throw things into the wastebasket while class is in session. When I asked why they would allow this kind of behavior, the teacher usually said they didn't know or that they didn't think it was important. How can students respect you if you don't respect yourself? If what you are saying is important, then you will expect the students to listen. If you don't expect them to listen, then what you are saying must not be important. In order to learn, students need structure and security. In fact, they demand it. You have been put there to establish it. If you don't, they will try to force you into providing it by misbehaving.

Respecting yourself is also crucial when dealing with parents. I am ashamed to say that too often the financial bottom line plays in here. I have even been told to consider parents and their children as "customers." How can we be Christian professional educators when we are asked to placate parents with issues in order to keep the money coming in? How can we respect ourselves as God's chosen instruments under those circumstances? Please don't fall into that trap. I have been an administrator and remember the challenges of keeping a school open, but there is no excuse for becoming a marketable commodity instead of offering a Christ-centered ministry.

Parents need to know that you are confident in your profession and not a hireling at their bidding. More importantly, they need to see your passion for the salvation of their child's soul. Respect yourself, knowing that you are doing the most important work possible for none other than God Himself.

An indication that we respect ourselves is the ability to admit our shortcomings. We are not perfect, and we accept the reality that we never will be. We are vulnerable to mistakes like everyone else. But our mistakes should not devastate us; as professionals, we learn from them and move on. When a challenging situation arises, take a quick inventory and make sure you understand what part of the problem is your piece; in other words, where does your responsibility lie? Once you understand that, correct what needs to be corrected and move on to help your students or colleagues. Don't allow your mistakes to trump your ability to do ministry.

Developing a "thick skin" will help to avoid taking everything personally. If you respect yourself, criticism is simply an opportunity to grow. In fact, invite evaluation and use it to become a more effective teacher. Knowing that you will not agree with everyone and everyone will not agree with you, use scripture as your guide, pray about it, make the best decision you can, and move on. Two people who respect themselves and each other can strongly disagree and still love each other in the Lord.

I gave the senior religion students a book to read with the intention of discussing it later in class. I had read the book previously but had forgotten a phrase in the book that was inappropriate for these students. When a few of the parents found that phrase in the book, the result was a strong negative reaction. A meeting was called so the concerned parents could voice their objection to the book. Not many showed up, but those who did used the occasion to challenge my general aptitude for teaching. They questioned my motives, methods, and content of the class. After listening for a while and watching my principal try to defend me, I realized they all had other issues on their plates. One parent's child had been molested at a young age. A different set of parents were disappointed in sending their child to our school and resented the Christian aspect altogether. Another family had control issues and resented anything that remotely infringed on their parental prowess or oversight.

I apologized for not rereading the book before I gave it to the students and told them I would collect the book and assign a different book. Then I gave them a quick run down of my credentials as a teacher. I laid out my whole program and the purpose behind it all. I informed them that I had spoken to a number of other pastors and other Christian teachers to see if my curriculum and methods were in line with our stated mission and ministry. I thanked them for their faithfulness to their children. I assured them that their children were safe under my tutelage and told them if they wanted to talk to me one-on-one, I would be glad to do so.

I know that if they had "smelled blood" by my being defensive, they would have continued to attack me and might have succeeded in running me out of the school. But when I displayed a confidence in my ministry to their children and a genuine love for them, the parents were totally disarmed. Truthfully, it was not a grievance worth being dismissed over, but that is what happens many times. A small thing gets blown out of proportion because we do not respect ourselves and the ministry we carry on for the Lord.

QUESTIONS FOR FURTHER DISCUSSION:

1. Define Christian professionalism as it relates to education.

_____

_____

_____

2. What in our culture works against us as Christian educators?

_____

_____

_____

3. How does the fact that the parents of our students pay tuition affect their attitude toward us as educators?

_____

_____

_____

4. How do you remain professional and at the same time show respect for student and parental opinion that differs from yours?

_____

_____

_____

5. What is the difference between not caring and having a "thick skin"?

_____

_____

_____

6. What would help administrators stop seeing parents and students as customers?

_____

_____

_____

7. How is respecting yourself not seeking your own glory? 7 "It is not good to eat much honey, nor is it glorious to seek one's own glory" (Pr. 25:2).

_____

_____

_____

8. How do people respect themselves and humble themselves at the same time? "Whoever exalts himself will be humbled, and whoever humbles himself will be exalted" (Mt. 23:12).

_____

_____

_____

More of God's Word on the Subject: II Corinthians 3:1-6, II Corinthians 10-12

CHAPTER 6

LOVE THE STUDENTS

The concept seems obvious, and yet I find that I have a hard time holding on to this foundational building block of *discipling* through discipline. Jesus' heart went out to all people. He often saw them as sheep without a shepherd. No matter how sinful they were, Jesus reached out in love as He did to the woman at the well, Zacchaeus the tax collector, Peter after he denied Him, and those crucifying Him, to name a few. He demonstrated that those who needed "discipline" were the ones He worked with the most. I, on the other hand, often wanted to write them off as losers who just made my life difficult. Once again we see that, for Jesus, it was always about the sinner's need and not His own, opposite to what I was doing.

Each one of our students is a child of God and is deeply and fully loved by Him. Ought we attempt to do any less? Our sin obviously keeps us from fulfilling this goal completely, but it is still our ultimate objective and we should continually pursue it. God has the ability to love the sinner while hating the sin, and by the power of the Holy Spirit we can do the same. True love expresses itself in a desire for the one we love to be in heaven. With that as the motivation, we should be able to get past frustrating behaviors and annoying traits and see the suffering soul beneath. This takes the selfishness out of our treatment of students.

When I was student teaching, I was not about to let the students get the best of me. Kenny was a rambunctious second grader. While observing my supervising teacher conduct class, I had pegged him as a troublemaker. The first day that I was in charge of the class, Kenny started squirming in his seat and then raised his hand emphatically. I tried to ignore him to teach him a lesson; after all, *I* was in charge *now*. When I did finally call on him, he asked if he could go to the bathroom. Being the all-knowing teacher I was, I said "No. You can wait until recess." He continued to squirm and then even more emphatically asked if he could go to the bathroom. I finally said he could go and as he made a dash for it, he vomited all over the floor and door. I will never forget how ashamed I was for not loving Kenny enough to put his need ahead of my need to *be in charge*. As I cleaned up the mess, I decided I would never prejudge a student's motives and would always look further into the situation before I made a decision.

Love is more an action than a feeling, as modeled by Jesus and His Father. If I say that I love my students, I need to do for them the things that will give them a better future. I have to keep doing things that leave no doubt in their minds that I love them and, more importantly, that Jesus loves them. This includes disciplining them when necessary.

An insight that I gained from John Bradshaw's book, *Healing the Shame That Binds You,* helped me practice this love. He observed that often times sexually abused people are overweight. He concluded that the real problem wasn't their weight, but the underlying problem of unresolved abuse. As teachers who love their students, we need to look deeper and realize that they are often dealing with serious problems that they can't leave at home no matter how hard they try. Just like the overweight person who eats the pain away, our students act out in order to deal with their issues. Few students misbehave without some provocation, direct or indirect.

Jesus looked into the broken hearts of the lost and helped them find healing in His love and forgiveness. He did not let their sin stop Him from reaching out to them. Our call is to offer our students the same love and forgiveness. We can't look into their hearts, but we *can* assume that there are deeper underlying problems that are motivating the unacceptable behavior. This is not a reason to excuse their behavior or a suggestion that there shouldn't be any consequences for their actions (See "CONSEQUENCES *plus* GRACE" appendix A). In fact, if you don't discipline them, you don't show love to them. The type of discipline we use, however, will determine if we are showing love or not. If we use their acting out as an opportunity to *disciple* them, then they will see the love that changes lives.

Love is shown in actions and not in feelings, but that does not mean that feelings are unimportant. One of the many facets of being created in His image is the gift of feelings. One of the most effective ways of showing love is to express our feelings and to help students express theirs. Feelings are not sinful in and of themselves. "Do not sin in your anger" (Eph. 4:26). Part of our *discipling* discipline is to help students recognize what feelings they are having and to encourage them to handle these feelings in a beneficial way. When we love someone, we give them permission to voice their fears, doubts, and frustrations in a non-judgmental environment.

Most communication *is* about feelings. We have trained children so often not to trust or talk about their feelings. Because of this, they are not in the practice of doing so. However, feelings will be communicated one way or another. If they can't express them verbally, they will make someone else feel the way they do by creating a situation that they think (rightly or wrongly) evokes the same feeling. This is where a lot of misbehavior comes from. But we can short circuit that by teaching them to describe their feeling in a constructive way.

The process of "Active Listening" gives students the opportunity to share their feelings. It is a great tool in showing love to students. Active listening is a non-judgmental, reflective give-and-take exchange that encourages the students to focus on their feelings. The statements "You feel _____ because_____" and "I feel _____ because _____" constitute the basic format for this exchange. We can help students by modeling the process when we are upset: "I feel insecure right now because I don't know why you are laughing. I am afraid you are laughing at me." That is so much more respectful and loving than demanding that, because of your insecurity, they stop laughing. If they don't show love in return by explaining their behavior or by stopping their laughing, confrontational discipline is needed. I strongly recommend if you are unfamiliar with the active listening process, that you take the time to study and practice it at length.

Loving our students creates an environment that allows them to be themselves without fear of evaluation or comparison. Christians shouldn't pit fellow Christians against one another. Too often we attempt to motivate students through shame by holding up one student as a being better than the others. This destroys community and sends the unintended message that people have differing value to us or to God because of what they do. God loves us all the same, regardless of what we do; that is grace. We have to be careful that our evaluation of students' work is only of their work and does not take on a personal bias. In our "human doing," as opposed to "human being," culture they get plenty of that already. If we believe that their value is not dependent on what they accomplish, then we will love them no matter how they are behaving or performing scholastically.

Please don't interpret my words as a syrupy sweet indulgent love. Jesus demonstrated tough love throughout His ministry. Real love does not look the other way when students are acting out. The truth of what they are doing must be held up to them in the mirror of the law. Your love is shown in the commitment to help them overcome their sin and the promise not to reject them because they remain sinners.

QUESTIONS FOR FURTHER DISCUSSION:

1. List five ways you can show love to your students outside the classroom.

_____

_____

_____

2. How does God's love for you help you love your students?

_____

_____

_____

3. What are your fears of getting into the area of feelings with students?

_____

_____

_____

4. Under what circumstances would you share your feelings with your students?

_____

_____

_____

5. Make five "Active Listening" statements to a partner.

_____

_____

_____

6. What is unloving about an out of control classroom?

_____

_____

_____

7. What is unloving about an overly controlled classroom?

_____

_____

_____

8. What makes it hard to see your students as brothers and sisters in Christ?
"Having purified your souls by your obedience to the truth for a sincere brotherly love, love one another earnestly from a pure heart" (I Peter 1:22).

_____

_____

_____

9. What gives us away when we don't love "earnestly?"

_____

_____

_____

10. How is Christian love different than love from non-Christians?
" ...and may the Lord make you increase and abound in love for one another and for all, as we do for you so that he may establish your hearts blameless in holiness before our God and Father, at the coming of our Lord Jesus with all his saints" (I Thess. 3:12-13).

_____

_____

_____

More of God's Word on the Subject: Matthew 9:36, Ephesians 6:12, John 20:21, James 2:1ff, Acts 10:34

CHAPTER 7

RESPECT THE STUDENTS

I used to teach a class for parents called "STEP—Systematic Training of Effective Parenting." One of the real strengths of the program was how clearly it taught parents to be respectful of their children. At the time, the way the program explained it was a new concept to me. Coming from a traditional German family, it took a while to understand what the concept of respecting children meant and to convince me that it wouldn't spoil children. I learned that respect is an essential part of the foundation of good discipline that leads to *discipling.*

With the understanding that students belong to God first and foremost, we realize we are only caregivers of His young people. We don't own them; they are entrusted to us for their training and nurturing. Please understand that I am not talking about doting on them or spoiling them. That is just as disrespectful. What I am saying is that they deserve the same kind of consideration we want given to us.

Our culture today is quickly losing its respect for the most vulnerable among us. Too often children are sacrificed on the altar of materialism and are abandoned, while their parents are busy amassing their "toys." In the meantime, children are raising themselves with TV and computers as the guiding light. The lack of value and respect for children cannot be more clearly demonstrated than by the fact that we can legally kill the children we don't want through abortion. With this as a backdrop to our profession, it is even more crucial that we show real respect for the precious souls put in our care.

Parents have temporarily handed part of their parental responsibility over to us as teachers. We are not our students' parents, however, and dare not see ourselves in that role. The roles of teacher and parent are distinctly and qualitatively different. It is disrespectful to think and act otherwise. Respecting students means you treat them as you would a guest whom you love and know well. Our role of teacher does not give us the right to shame, berate, or treat students like our possessions. You would never embarrass guests by mocking them or by making decisions without considering their feelings. Using possessive terms like "my kids," "my classroom," kills community and shows a lack of respect for the students.

Can you even imagine an adult friend of yours walking in with dirty feet and your screaming at him/her, "Get off of my clean floor! What is the matter with you? Were you born in a barn?" But with children we have somehow given ourselves license to treat them with a different set of rules. Consider the comparison: How many of your friends ask for your permission to go to the bathroom? Could students just tell you where they are going like your friends do when they leave a room? And could you then only discipline the one or two who abuse the privilege? I am suggesting that it would be much more respectful to treat them in this manner.

From a Christian perspective, children are our equals. Their bodies, like ours, are the temples of the Holy Spirit. They have the same purpose in life as we do. We are co-heirs of the same heaven. Our role as teacher or administrator does not change that. They are people for whom Jesus died. They are not monsters in disguise. I must confess that I have caught myself in conversations with other teachers that I would never want students to hear. As our spiritual equals, it is entirely appropriate to ask a student for forgiveness when we mess up, just as we would from another adult. We serve them just as Jesus served others—sometimes with gentle words and sometimes with *discipling* discipline.

Our school has a tradition of the "senior prank." I was asked by some seniors if I could help them with their prank by unlocking the school. I was assured that nothing malicious or destructive would happen. I believed them, let them in, and then went to my room and worked for an hour or so. Unbeknownst to the other pranksters, one of them had brought a power pack screwdriver. Every screw he saw he loosened. What a mess! When I discovered this, I fixed everything I could and straightened up the other prank aftermath, too. The next day I spoke to the principal, confessing my lack of judgment and asking for her forgiveness. Then I asked for permission to speak to the whole student body. I stood in front of 300 students and asked for forgiveness from them. I admitted that my desire to seek acceptance from the seniors had clouded my judgment and had shown disrespect to the faculty and rest of the student body.

God blessed what could have been a disaster with a stronger community, an understanding of forgiveness, a feeling of equality among His people and a deeper respect for my role as teacher by the students.

We need to contemplate what respect in the classroom looks like. When you start class, do you demand that the students quiet down immediately, or do you give them time to finish a sentence or two first? If the classroom is all about you, they need to stop mid- sentence. But if you respect them, you indicate in a non-threatening way that you are about to begin class and then give them 30 seconds or so to finish up what they are saying. Their social lives are important to them and therefore should be important to you, as well. Obviously, there will be one or two who will try to take advantage of your grace time, but that is when you use the discipline of confrontation which we will get into later.

Allowing as much freedom as is age-appropriate and healthy for effective instruction is a way of communicating to our students that we respect and trust them. Again, I am not talking about abdicating your responsibility as a teacher; however, giving them choices empowers them. Could they choose their own seats on occasion, subsequently moving those who can't control their talking because they are sitting next to their best friends? They feel powerless in so many areas of their lives already, why add your classroom to the list?

As a result of Christ's victory and the gift of faith from the Holy Spirit, God has restored the condition of having choices like Adam and Eve had before the fall. God has freely empowered His people, and we have no right to take that away from our students. Our job is to educate them about which choices are beneficial and which are not. Certainly in the role of teacher you will have all kinds of expectations, but those expectations should not go beyond the boundaries of the teacher-pupil relationship.

When we nit-pick students about things like dress code, keeping their desks in a straight line, tying their shoes, or sitting up in their seats, we end up majoring in minors and the students resent it. Unless they see a connection between our rules and what matters to them, rules are just rules. I have continually grown in my appreciation of God's rules as I discover how all of them come from His unfailing love for us. He doesn't *need* us to obey any of them. They are for us, not Him. The rules of our classroom and school should be the same. If the rules are in place only to keep *us* happy while restricting the students' choices, then we disrespect our students and take away the freedom God has given them.

Students are more likely to accept and then obey classroom rules if they understand why you have established the rules. After a few weeks of school, revisit your rules with the students and discuss what is working and what is not. If they have learned to trust you, they will be more likely to give their honest opinions about the effectiveness of your rules. I would love to see student council members, at an age-appropriate level, have serious input into the school wide rules.

The discipline we use for misbehavior should have a logical connection to the behavior we are trying to correct. If there is no connection, the child realizes that our "discipline" is simply punishment. "What does staying in for recess have to do with whispering to a classmate during instruction?" they ask. Wouldn't a more logical consequence be a move to a different seat or an explanation of why talking in class is not good for the community?

God doesn't punish; rather He allows the natural consequences of our choices to discipline us. We discover quite quickly that when we disobey Him, life doesn't work. We willingly return to an obedient life because it is just easier that way—it makes sense. Our schools and classrooms should, as much as possible, generate the same result. Punishment does not get willing adherence to rules; instead it creates resentment.

It is disrespectful to train students with punishments and rewards like you would an animal. Giving treats to "good" students while the "bad" students have to watch them enjoy the treats, only serves to destroy community. It teaches the wrong motivation for giving God glory with their lives. If our desire is to *disciple* our students, we must, like God, treat them all the same when it come to blessings. "You have heard that it was said, 'You shall love your neighbor and hate your enemy.' [44] But I say to you, Love your enemies and pray for those who persecute you, [45] so that you may be sons of your Father who is in heaven. For he makes his sun rise on the evil and on the good, and sends rain on the just and on the unjust" (Matthew 5:43-45).

All rules, policies, and practices have to be in clear agreement with Scripture, and punishment for punishment's sake should not exist. God does not punish His children; the punishment we deserve was placed on Jesus when He went to the cross. Instead, God disciplines us. He instructs us in His Word, revealing which choices would be the most beneficial. If we do the same in our classrooms, we help our students mature with a sense of independence that will serve them well as they move on in life. If we don't, in other words, if we decide everything for them, they develop a self image that says they are not capable of making decisions for themselves.

We must resist the attitude that because we are the teachers, we are the only determinant in the room. Our students may have better ideas from time to time about what may make a more effective learning environment. Respect the ideas of the students. Get excited when they come up with something you had not thought of. Respect their opinions even if they are far-fetched. Take the time to work through the logic of any faulty thinking in a respectful way, and look for value even in flawed ideas. Help them bounce their suggestions off Scripture. If you simply tell them they are wrong, you lose the chance to teach them how to evaluate their ideas.

Being respected is empowering. God respected us enough to entrust us with His message of salvation. Think of the disciples we will be sending out into the world if they have been taught that their ideas matter, that they can make good choices, and that they have much to offer. This confidence comes from being respected at home and at school.

QUESTIONS FOR FURTHER DISCUSSION:

1. What rules do you have in your school and classroom that could unnecessarily take choices away from the students?

_____

_____

_____

2. Why might parents encourage you to establish controlling rules in your school and classroom?

_____

_____

_____

3. Which of your consequences for unacceptable behavior are punitive in nature?

_____

_____

_____

4. List your ten favorite "labels" for students and then categorize them as respectful or disrespectful.

_____

_____

_____

5. What is the difference between catering to children and respecting them?

_____

_____

_____

6. How does this passage help you respect your students? "In the presence of God and of Christ Jesus and of the elect angels I charge you to keep these rules without prejudging, doing nothing from partiality" (I Tim. 5:21).

_____

_____

_____

7. What are some of the prejudgments you have been guilty of in the past?

_____

_____

_____

8. Could "young nor old" be rightly added here? Why or why not? "There is neither Jew nor Greek, there is neither slave nor free, there is neither male nor female, for you are all one in Christ Jesus" (Gal. 3:28).

_____

_____

_____

9. How should this passage be applied to teaching? "Whoever causes one of these little ones who believe in me to sin, it would be better for him if a great millstone were hung around his neck and he were thrown into the sea" (Mark 9:42).

_____

_____

_____

10. What joyful message in the following passage can you share with your students and use in your *discipling*? "Now before faith came, we were held captive under the law, imprisoned until the coming faith would be revealed. [24] So then, the law was our guardian until Christ came, in order that we might be justified by faith" (Galatians 3:23-24).

_____

_____

_____

More of God's Word on the Subject: Matthew 23:9, Romans 12:19, Hebrews 12

CHAPTER 8

BUILD COMMUNITY

S cripture teaches that one of our greatest weapons against Satan is the "fellowship of believers." One of Satan's favorite tools is to convince us through isolation that we struggle alone in the world and that no one understands or cares about us. When we don't build community in our classrooms, we give Satan additional access to our students.

One of my favorite disciplining tools, before I realized how damaging it was to students, was to isolate them. Making them look foolish or even physically separating them from the other students would almost always get them under control. It not only hurt the misbehaving student, but it set the other students against me for hurting their community—I was now the enemy. Isolation gets control but undermines *discipling*. When discipline includes community building, battle lines are eliminated. Community fosters cooperation, fellowship, and willing obedience; it provides opportunity for *discipling*.

To understand community, we need to first understand the concept of roles. In our culture today, roles are being compromised, challenged, and confused. In the typical sit-com, the male role is mocked, children are raising their parents, and women are encouraged to be as male-like as they possibly can. When we disregard roles or alter them, we suffer as a people.

God established roles to maintain community. We see God's love in that no one role is more important than another, as illustrated by Jesus' washing of the disciples' feet. Administrators are no more important than preschoolers. They just have different roles. This is not to say that roles cannot fluctuate under certain circumstances. They do not need to be rigid and unchanging to be effective. But we accept appropriate roles as a way to ensure the community's continuing success (See "LUTHER ON RANK AND SUPERIORITY "Appendix B").

Jesus doesn't want us to lord our role as teacher or administrator over the students like the Gentiles. "But Jesus called them to him and said, 'You know that the rulers of the Gentiles lord it over them, and their great ones exercise authority over them. [26] It shall not be so among you. But whoever would be great among you must be your servant, [27] and whoever would be first among you must be your slave, [28] even as the Son of Man came not to be served but to serve, and to give his life as a ransom for many" (Matt. 20:25-28). Fellowship is lost when we change roles into positions of power. The loss of the common good pits Christian against Christian, something God never intended.

If we can get our students to understand this and they see how community works in our classrooms, the need for discipline will be cut significantly. When students see us pulling for them and using our role as teachers to help them become the best children of God they can be, most of them will be more than willing to work with us instead of against us.

Even the youngest of students realize that in any group trying to accomplish a goal, there have to be different roles and responsibilities. When we teach them to respect our role and they see that we respect theirs, community works. We accomplish this when our actions, words, and attitudes are all in sync.

From a very young age students need to learn the difference between the roles needed at home and the roles needed in school. They should see the difference between teacher and parent, and among classmates, siblings, and neighborhood friends. All students, young and old, are helped when they understand the distinct community the classroom is and what roles are necessary for this community to function effectively and accomplish its goals. Thus rules do vary as they pertain to different settings.

Building on our common faith, we can develop a spiritual intimacy in the classroom that can be found only among Christians. When we use the building blocks of this *discipling* process, we create an atmosphere of safety and security which will foster a communal concern in the classroom: student to student, teacher to student, and student to teacher. This ultimately spills out into the hallways, gym, and lunchroom.

One of the aspects of this community is trust. When there is genuine Christian love and respect, a natural outgrowth is the increase of trust in each other. Remember how you developed trust with a new friend? It took time and many experiences to determine if he/she could really be trusted. When a community is working well, trust is being developed and more can be asked of each other without too much explanation. If it is not working, everything is questioned and second guessed. We cannot assume that our students trust us just because we are the teacher or the adult. They have had sufficient encounters with enough people to realize that not all can be trusted. We will have to earn their trust, just as they have to earn ours. I know that the process I am presenting builds up trust very quickly. When a situation occurs that forces you to ask for the student's trust it will be there, and you will have plenty to use and some left over to build on for the next challenging situation. Use your trust account wisely. Phrases like, "You will just have to trust me on this one" or "Because I said so!" or "Because I am the teacher and you are the student" should be used sparingly. The more successful you are at the *discipling* discipline, the slower you will deplete the trust you have built up with your students. In successful communities individuals trust each other.

When community has been established and an undesirable situation occurs, we can rally *as* a community to fix it. It should sound something like this: "Stop! This is not working! **WE** need to figure out a better way of doing this. What can **WE** do to make this work better for **EVERYONE**? What is God telling **US** to do here? How can "**WE**" improve "**OUR**" school?"

Teachers cannot just give this lip service. Students know when you are trying to manipulate them into compliance with what you have already decided they should do.

The importance of community is another one of those principles that is in direct opposition to the culture of the day. In our culture the individual is more important than the community. Again and again, our society protects the rights of the individual at the expense of the community. Our most devastating, anti-Biblical practices are a result of this individualistic thinking—abortion, gay marriage, couples living together before marriage—to mention a few. We have not stopped to look at the impact on the whole because the individual's rights supersede the health of the community.

God has never isolated His people or asked them to function only as individuals. The only one who was asked to do that was Jesus on the cross. "My God, My God, why have You forsaken me?" (Mark 15:34) From Adam on He has established community for our benefit. "It is not good that man should be alone" (Gen. 2:18). He established nations in service to their citizens. His covenants have always been for the good of all. His laws are all given as a protection for the individual *and* the community. I can't think of one rule or guideline that is for the individual alone. Even the solitary practice of personal prayer is for the benefit of others in the community.

If we want the benefit of God's wisdom and His understanding of human nature, we will establish community school wide. We will make every effort to develop common goals among all parties involved. We will do all in our power to eliminate the "we/they" rift that so often exists between students and faculty, and faculty and administration, for that matter. This is not too difficult to accomplish when we love and respect ourselves and the students.

QUESTIONS FOR FURTHER DISCUSSION:

1. What evidence do you see in our culture that we do not value community?

_____

_____

_____

2. What evidence is there that individual rights have now become more important than the health of the community?

_____

_____

_____

3. What are the advantages of belonging to the Christian community?

_____

_____

_____

4. What are some classroom weaknesses that make building community difficult?

_____

_____

_____

5. Why do roles not get lost or confused in a successful community?

_____

_____

_____

6. How does this passage apply to the classroom and the school at large? "I therefore, a prisoner for the Lord, urge you to walk in a manner worthy of the calling to which you have been called, [2] with all humility and gentleness, with patience, bearing with one another in love, [3] eager to maintain the unity of the Spirit in the bond of peace. [4] There is one body and one Spirit—just as you were called to the one hope that belongs to your call— ..." (Eph. 4:1-4).

_____

_____

_____

7. Describe a situation where you saw real Christian community in action.

_____

_____

_____

8. How do you know whether your students trust you or not?

_____

_____

_____

9. How do these verses fit the whole school environment and help with the understanding of roles? "For just as the body is one and has many members, and all the members of the body, though many, are one body, so it is with Christ. [22] On the contrary, the parts of the body that seem to be weaker are indispensable, [26] If one member suffers, all suffer together; if one member is honored, all rejoice together" (I Cor. 12:12,22,26).

_____

_____

_____

10. Discuss the statement "No harmony equals no Christian love." "And above all these put on love, which binds everything together in perfect harmony" (Col. 3:14).

_____

_____

_____

11. What good news about community does Paul give us in this passage? "So then you are no longer strangers and aliens, but you are fellow citizens with the saints and members of the household of God, [20] built on the foundation of the apostles and prophets, Christ Jesus himself being the cornerstone" (Ephes. 2:19-20).

_____

_____

_____

More of God's Word on the Subject: Ephesians 2:11ff, Acts 2-5, Mark 4:26-29, Matthew 13, II Corinthians 3:1-6, I Corinthians 12:14ff, Acts 2-5

CHAPTER 9

USE LAW AND GOSPEL

The two basic doctrines of the Bible are law and gospel. To be faithful to God and His Word we need to understand these two concepts and use them in proper balance. I do not profess to have this completely in hand as a doctrine or claim to always use it effectively in the classroom. It is a constant struggle to get it right. But I do know that striving for that balance is essential in maintaining a Christian environment and being an effective *discipler*. The simple definition that I was taught in confirmation class is as follows: The law shows us our sin and God's wrath, and the Gospel shows us our Savior and God's Grace. How and when to use each doctrine is a constant challenge to the Christian educator.

I am assuming that you are reading this because you are a Christian teacher of Christians and some non-Christians in a Christian setting. If some of your students have not been saved by the gift of faith through the Holy Spirit, you will want to know who they are. You will use the law and gospel in a different way with them. I will have some suggestions about our ministry to them a little later. In regard to the Christian students, we can start with the assumption that they no longer need to be introduced to the law. The Christian students know the solution to their sin. They accept that they are sinners and that God demands perfection as presented in His Word. But because they trust in the forgiveness won for them by Jesus, the law has now become a gift that protects and guides them through life. We do not need to drive them to the cross out of fear. Continual reminders of the Godly standards found in Scripture are certainly appropriate and helpful. The part I think we too often miss is that the law should also remind them how much God loves them—how much He has sacrificed to save them from their sin. *Discipling* discipline teaches them that no matter how hard they try, they will continue to sin and remain in constant need of a Savior.

The Christian educator helps the student see God's love in the law. Students should be nurtured and educated about how to live out their sanctified lives. We have the privilege of showing them how obedience to God is the best way to find joy and peace in this life and that the natural consequence of sin is painful. That is one of the processes in *discipling*.

If we as teachers and administrators treat young Christians as unregenerate heathen, we are not representing God accurately. Our treatment of sin and its consequences should look totally different than that of a non-Christian school. If we love and respect our students as fellow Christians, our discipline will reflect a proper balance of law and gospel while recognizing and respecting their confession of faith in Jesus

(See "WHO DO YOU THINK YOU'RE TALKING TO?" appendix C).

Observe in scripture how differently Jesus dealt with repentant sinners as compared to the unrepentant. The woman at the well, the publican, the tax collector, and the prostitute all received God's mercy as repentant sinners. Conversely, the hardhearted, stiff-necked scribes, Pharisees, priests, and Roman rulers were taken to task in no uncertain terms. But for the most part, our use of the law should be an opportunity to help students grow. It becomes a tool to build up, not tear down.

The apostle Paul talks at length about our freedom from the law. He encourages the church leaders not to put their people back under the yoke of the law. "For freedom Christ has set us free; stand firm therefore, and do not submit again to a yoke of slavery" (Galatians 5:1-2). He openly states that we are free to do *anything*; that all things are permissible to the Christian. But he is quick to remind us to ask if our actions are beneficial. "'All things are lawful,' but not all things are helpful. 'All things are lawful,' but not all things build up. [24] Let no one seek his own good, but the good of his neighbor" (I Cor. 10:23-24).

To the Christian, the law stops being God's tool for judgment and becomes His guide for a fulfilling life. Our students need to practice their freedoms; our classrooms can become the laboratories where this is done. Once we realize that the gospel through the Holy Spirit has regenerative power, we will not rely on the law to control. We will instead help the students tap into the gospel as a changing force in their lives, using the law as a tool to guide their choices.

I recently overheard a veteran teacher announce, "I am proud to say I have only one rule in my classroom—respect." I agree with that approach. Respecting God and your neighbor is a good balance of law and gospel. It affords freedom and yet asks for self-discipline. It gives opportunity to intervene when troubles arise, helping students make good choices. I know that this teacher's classroom is never in chaos, nor are the students disrespectful. He covers his material in a timely fashion, and the students like the atmosphere of his classroom.

Now concerning the lost students that may be in your school. Our treatment and expectations of them are different from the Christian students. We cannot look into the heart of each child and know who is saved and who is not, or who the hypocrites are among us. That is not our job—we leave that to God. However, we can base our actions on the public confessions they make. If a student does not confess Jesus as Lord and Savior, we can address that student with certain principles in mind. First, because of natural knowledge, heathens live in constant fear of a holy God who will one day call them into account. Some acknowledge this fear, but others pretend that it has no effect on them. However, all people sense that God will use the law written on their hearts and scripture, if they have heard it, to judge them.

Second, unbelievers desperately need to hear the solution to this hopeless dilemma. Our job is to drive them to the cross through the law so that they can see the gospel and then receive the gift of faith. I was showing a film about the end times that related how many signs were pointing to the fact that the world will end soon. I opened the class up for discussion, and a student who had previously said she didn't believe in Jesus commented that I wasn't going to scare her into believing. I told her I was doing my best with the law to do just that. Neither the film nor I had said anything about judgment or heaven or hell. Nevertheless, her conscience and the law written on her heart were scaring her. The film simply made it more imminent and real for her. I had the opportunity to present the gospel to her and offer the hope in Jesus Christ.

Third, when disciplining the unregenerate, we cannot expect obedience through *discipleship* which would be a repentance of faith. Punishment is therefore appropriate because there is no motivation coming from a love for Jesus to change their behavior or to help the community of believers. To draw from an empty well is futile. Until they do come to faith, the best we can hope for is either 1) compliance in order to avoid punishment or 2) the desire to stay out of trouble because of the negative consequence misbehavior brings.

As stated earlier, however, punishment or fear created through the law is never appropriate for the regenerate child of God. As you can see, the basic difference is motivation. We attempt to motivate the Christian students to be good *disciples* because of their love for Jesus, while the motivation for the unregenerate is fear of God's wrath if they are not obedient.

QUESTIONS FOR FURTHER DISCUSSION:

1. Why is the balance of Law/Gospel so hard to keep?

_____

_____

_____

2. How do these two doctrines affect your personal life?

_____

_____

_____

3. How can you incorporate the three uses of the Law in your classroom — Mirror, Rule, and Curb?

_____

_____

_____

4. What fears arise as you think about giving freedom to your students?

_____

_____

_____

5. What aspects of your school or classroom rules put the yoke of the law back on your students?

_____

_____

_____

6. How could this verse be applied to the classroom? "Brothers, if anyone is caught in any transgression, you who are spiritual should restore him in a spirit of gentleness. Keep watch on yourself, lest you too be tempted. [2] Bear one another's burdens, and so fulfill the law of Christ" (Gal. 6:1-2).

_____

_____

_____

7. Is "any transgression" (Gal. 6:1) different from a student's disobedience? Why or why not?

_____

_____

_____

8. Describe the "law of Christ" (Gal. 6:2) in terms of the gospel.

_____

_____

_____

More of God's Word on the Subject: Psalm 119, I Timothy 1:8ff, Romans 2:12

CHAPTER 10

CHECK YOUR MOTIVES

One of the pitfalls that destroys the whole *discipling*/discipline process is wrong motives. Even with the best intentions and dedication to our students, Satan works overtime to sabotage our efforts. Time in the classroom has a tendency to wear us down to the point of survival mode. That is when motives get off track. We feel the pressures of time restraints, parental expectations, administrators' evaluations, timely coverage of the subject matter, and on and on it goes. We easily lose track of the real reason we are in the classroom in the first place. If we are not in a good place as individuals, it is easy to see how we can slip into motives that are not generated by our love for Jesus and the students.

One of the most reoccurring negative motives is control for the sake of one's own sanity. The focus shifts to ourselves just so we can get through the day, and discipline is used to keep things quiet and manageable. The classroom becomes all about us and no longer about the students. Our decisions, then, have nothing to do with their eternal life, but rather with our comfort zone and how much we can tolerate. Discipline then only stops unwanted behavior but doesn't change a student's attitude and heart.

If this goes on long enough, we develop a "we against them" mentality. Our motive then turns into "thwarting the enemies' tactics, which we all know are meant to destroy us." We are convinced there is a conspiracy headed up by young "ne'er do wells" whose plan is to take over the school at any minute. I have often caught myself in the teachers' lounge or lunchroom talking about students in a most disrespectful way. Teachers have a tendency to put their heads together and strategize ways to control the enemy—their students. This ultimately weakens our attempts at *discipling*. What we really need to do, teachers and students alike, is redirect our efforts toward defeating the real enemy, Satan.

The desire for power is an addictive source of wrong motive. I don't like to admit that there were times in my ministry that the sense of power in the classroom or as an administrator went to my head. Administrators are especially susceptible to this temptation. Absolute power corrupts absolutely except, of course, in God's case. In our own little kingdom of the classroom or the school office it is easy to usurp power that was never intended to be given. Too often the checks and balances that were established to protect the student or fellow staff members have failed, and the power junkies get out of control. Students have often told me how they can see right through this wrong motive and know that the discipline was just a ruse to exert power (my words, not theirs).

Fear and insecurity also drive many disciplinary actions. In fear that the students are secretly laughing at us behind our backs, we lash out in unfounded suspicion at every smirk we see. This is why loving and respecting ourselves is so important; and if they are laughing at us, so what? They are the students—we are the well prepared professional adults.

I have taught with well meaning Spiritually alive Christians who wanted to serve their Lord and chose teaching His children as the way to do that. However, they had neither the skill nor the gift for teaching. In their frustration they blamed the children and used discipline as a way of relieving their frustrations. It is really just a matter of misdirected zeal for serving God. For the sake of the students and themselves, these types of folks need to find a different way to serve the God they love or develop both the outlook and skills to work effectively with young people.

Unfulfilled dreams of childhood can motivate teachers to "go back to school" and be successful this time. Students *have* to accept their teachers, don't they? The teacher can now be BMOCs or BWOCs (Big Man/Woman on Campus). This often precipitates a lack of discipline because they are looking for acceptance or love "in all the wrong faces." Both *discipling* and discipline are too threatening to these teachers because these actions may alienate the students and leave the misdirected teachers on the outs again, just like the first time they went to school as children or teens. I have seen the same thing in single parents who don't want to lose the companionship of the only people they are close to—their children.

I am sure you can add more to this list of negative motives for disciplining or teaching in general. The point is that wrong motives for teaching or disciplining make us ineffective and destroy our mission of *discipling*.

Loving service to Jesus and His people is the only motive given in Scripture. Washing His disciples' feet was a total role reversal in Jesus' day. If anyone deserved having others serve Him, it was Jesus. But instead He came to serve us: ". . . even as the Son of Man came not to be served but to serve, and to give his life as a ransom for many" (Matt. 20:28).

With that as our perfect model of right motivation, led by the Holy Spirit, we can enjoy a meaningful and effective ministry *discipling* our students.

QUESTIONS FOR FURTHER DISCUSSION:

1. What negative motives have you been guilty of?

_____

_____

_____

2. List three Bible passages that help you to keep your motives for Christian teaching clear.

_____

_____

_____

3. How does your school's mission and ministry statement help you to establish and maintain clear motives for your teaching?

_____

_____

_____

4. How does the love and respect for yourself affect your motives in the classroom?

_____

_____

_____

5. Can a teacher's motives be God pleasing and still have undesirable results? If so, why? If not, why not?

_____

_____

_____

6. What are some methods that help you determine your motives for choosing Christian teaching as a profession?

_____

_____

_____

7. What good news do you hear as St. Paul struggles with his service to God in this passage? "So I find it to be a law that when I want to do right, evil lies close at hand. [22] For I delight in the law of God, in my inner being, [23] but I see in my members another law waging war against the law of my mind and making me captive to the law of sin that dwells in my members. [24] Wretched man that I am! Who will deliver me from this body of death? [25] Thanks be to God through Jesus Christ our Lord! So then, I myself serve the law of God with my mind, but with my flesh I serve the law of sin" (Romans 7:21-25).

_____

_____

_____

More of God's Word on the Subject: Ephesians 6:12

CHAPTER 11

CONFRONT: ASK "WHY?"

If all the other building blocks are in place, and you have built community in your classroom, you will not have to use a confrontational process very often. Under certain circumstances, however, and at your discretion, you may have to deal with situations that call for strong disciplinary intervention.

Confrontation and helping students become more accountable for their actions is the pivotal point of my whole thesis on discipline. This is the step that I feel most teachers do not take. Please hear me out as I try to explain just what I mean by confrontation as it relates to discipline and *discipling*. At first it sounds like it would take too much time and is too personal an approach. I assure you that this type of process will pay off in the end and will not be contrary to any of the objectives mentioned previously. Confrontation may sound like a strong word when dealing with students, but this is not a combative type of interaction. Instead, it is simply a clear, direct and intentional approach of *discipling* while disciplining. Confrontation does not exclude gentleness as asked for in scripture. " . . .with all humility and gentleness, with patience, bearing with one another in love," (Ephesians. 4:2) and "Brothers, if anyone is caught in any transgression, you who are spiritual should restore him in a spirit of gentleness" (Galatians 6:1a). But gentleness is coupled with action and intervention, and I believe it must include confrontation as well.

As I look to Scripture for guidance and to Jesus as the perfect example, I find a process that He used repeatedly as He disciplined and *discipled* His listeners. In the book of Matthew alone, He *confronts* those He is disciplining and *discipling* ten times with the question, **"WHY?"** He asks them to examine their lives in order to discover the motivations for their actions or beliefs. The three other gospels repeat and/or add others with only a few less than Matthew: Mark includes eight; Luke—nine; and John—seven (See appendix D). The Bible does not tell us if those He confronted actually took the time to figure out their motives, but it is certainly clear that it is an important step toward repentance and restoration for the sinner. Asking "why?' is not the only method Jesus used, but it seems to me to be the most applicable to the classroom setting.

I must admit that I stumbled on to this quite by accident. After spending countless hours as a pastoral counselor, I realized that unless we understand *why* we do the things we do, we have little hope of changing our behaviors. Using that knowledge when I returned to the classroom, I discovered that asking "why?" was the most effective way to *disciple* and discipline students at the same time. It was respectful to me and to the students. It showed them genuine love and concern.

If you desire to *disciple* your students and not just stop undesirable behavior, then this is worth your time and effort. When Jesus confronted people with the question "why?", He knew the answer before He posed the question. Obviously, it was for their good that He asked it. We do the same thing when we confront our students by asking them to try to understand *why* they are doing what they are doing. We are seeking their good and not ours.

This is where loving and respecting your students will make a difference. As your motivation becomes clear to them, they will be more willing to share what is going on in their lives that may be precipitating the undesirable behavior. You will have the opportunity to apply the Word of God to the situation, all of which would have been lost if you had just stopped the behavior with punishment, isolation, or sarcasm.

Ever since I came upon this process, I never "punished" a confessed Christian student as I had in my earlier teaching experiences. I am comfortable with the fact that I have never written a referral in sixteen years of teaching high school. Still, my classroom is one of the more orderly rooms in the building. My belief is that if I am not willing to *disciple* students, I have no right to punish them either.

That is not to say I have never had situations that I chose to handle outside the classroom. I have even taken a student to the office and informed the principal that the student was not to enter my classroom again until I had spoken with his parents. He had openly and disrespectfully defied my role as teacher. He wanted nothing to do with our community. When I tried to *disciple* him, asking why he was doing what he was doing, he basically laughed at me. This was a person who needed the law.

The only students that this system does not work with are those who are steadfastly rejecting the community you are trying to establish or those who are under the influence or are controlled by their addiction to drugs or alcohol. However, these students make up a small minority in most Christian schools. Even the non-Christian student will benefit and change behavior through confrontation, but their motivation for obedience and your motivation for confronting will be different, as explained in the law/gospel chapter.

I found that the time I spent with *discipling* my students early in the school year was gained back ten times over by the end of the year. When all the building blocks of this system are in place and the confrontation is used a few times, students develop better tools in self control and make better choices. Confrontational discipline also establishes for you a reputation that precedes you. As new students come to your classroom, the time needed to establish this process is minimized.

Before I give you an example and a quick outline of the process I use, let me explain that I am not advocating only one approach to confrontational *discipling*/discipline. This is a process that I have developed over the years as a result of my experiences, personality, skills, and interests. You will need to develop yours, as well. The important elements of the process are that it is intentional, that it helps the students become accountable for their actions, and that it is directed at trying to understand why they are acting the way they are acting. It should not just stop behavior.

Remember Chris from Chapter Two "Teach and Discipline"? At that time, I chose to use his situation as an opportunity to establish who I would be as their teacher. I was sitting in one of the student desks in the circle I had formed before the students came to class. I stayed in my seat and waited for things to quiet down a little. I began to talk, and some students continued to visit and ignored my attempt at getting started. Chris was one of those continuing their conversations. I chose not to shout over the noise or to give dirty looks to the ones not settling down. I stood up and again attempted to start class. Most of them, at that point, quieted down, indicating they were ready to begin. Chris, however, was still joking around with his buddies, but not as loudly as before. I walked over to Chris and stood near his desk, introducing myself and the overall content of the class.

As I continued to talk, so did Chris. I then stopped and gave myself time to pray and get my thoughts together. I stood in front of Chris and asked him why I could not expect him to quiet down along with the rest of the students. I asked him to explain to me and to the class why he was acting the way he was. He sort of laughed and then said he was sorry and that I should continue. I told him that I would rather work at understanding him than to get to the lesson. He laughed again. I assured him that I was serious and that I was concerned about his behavior and about him. I told him that there is a reason for everything we do and there is a reason why he was unwilling to quiet down when he saw me trying to start class. I asked the class if I had given them sufficient time to finish their conversations before starting and most of them agreed that I had.

As an example of every action having a reason, I asked why he was wearing a hat in class when as a senior he was well aware of the rules. He said he didn't know. I assured him that he did but that he might not want to admit to it aloud. I asked his permission for the rest of us to make some guesses for him. He agreed. I said maybe he had a bad haircut or that a certain girl liked the hat. Then I asked the other students if they had any suggestions as to why Chris was disobeying the rules.

By this time Chris was ready to drop the whole thing and said he would take it off if it bothered me that much. I informed him that the hat didn't bother me at all, but that I was sincerely concerned as to why he chose to start our relationship in such a defiant manner. The other students told me that this was just who Chris was and that he was always like this. I asked Chris if this was true, and he nodded in assent. I asked him again why he was like this. He said again he didn't know. Then he asked if I could just "drop it already" and move on. I told him I cared too much about his future to just drop it. I tried to convince him that I was genuinely concerned and that it would be vital to him that he understand himself enough to know why he did the things he did.

I told him that I understood that he didn't know me well enough yet to trust me, but I hoped that that would change. I then said that I guessed that the hat was a test to see what kind of teacher I was going to be and that he needed the attention of the class to feel good about himself. He sat quietly for a few seconds and said, "Maybe." I knew this was as good an answer as I was going to get on the first day of class so I let it go at that.

But then the other students started asking why I was making such a big deal out of just wearing a hat in class. They wondered aloud why I didn't just tell him to take it off. I asked them in return what that would have accomplished and how that would have helped Chris. I explained that I wanted to work *with* them not against them. I promised that I would respect them in their role as students and hoped they would respect me in mine as teacher.

Chris never wore his hat in class again. Whenever I started class, he quieted down quickly, and he was always honest with me when we had discussions in class. We usually didn't agree on things, but he wasn't afraid to disagree because he did learn to trust me.

This encounter took a lot more time than if I had just told him to take his hat off and quiet down. He probably would have reluctantly obeyed but then chalked me up as another teacher who just wanted to control the classroom and could care less about what was really going on inside the students. Had I done that, I would not have *discipled* him. As it was, the door was opened to continue the dialogue of making better choices. I found out through later discussions that Chris was neglected by his parents. He had total freedom. He could stay out as late as he wanted any night of the week. He could stay at a friend's house and not tell his parents where he was. Chris was crying out for structure in his life and hoped that I would give it to him. The sad thing was that when people tried to control Chris, he would rebel, making his and everyone else's lives around him miserable.

When Chris discovered that I really cared about him as a person, he didn't know how to react. Most of the adults he had dealt with had either ignored him, writing him off as hopeless, or had clamped down on him with rules and control tactics, neither of which helped Chris grow in becoming a *disciple* of Jesus. As I mentioned before, Chris would stop in from time to time to talk about choices in his life, and I could tell he was working at becoming a true *disciple* of his Savior. Sadly, he later made many more bad decisions. A person doesn't overcome a life of neglect in one school year. But Chris had learned to ask himself the question "Why?" He knew that at least one person loved him enough to hold him accountable for his actions.

The process works something like this. When a student acts out in such a way that a glance or two doesn't change his/her behavior, walk closer to them and continue doing whatever you were doing. If the behavior continues, decide if the actions are of a private or public nature. If the behavior is more private, you should establish a time when you can pursue the *discipling*/discipline with him/her privately, using many of the same ideas.

If the student's behavior is of a more public nature that is affecting the community, say a quick prayer, then begin. Describe what you have just observed in some detail. Ask if he/she agrees that it was an unhealthy or disruptive way to act. Ask the student why he/she is choosing to behave in that manner.

One of the principles upon which this system is built is that everything we do is a choice. The perfect free will God gave us when He created us in His image was lost and limited when Adam and Eve fell into sin. We are now bound to the sinful will, but that does not mean we have stopped making choices. It simply means we don't have the ability to make choices with the right motives.

By the power of the Holy Spirit, Christians can and do make good choices. Teachers are privileged to help students learn how to make God pleasing decisions and to avoid the negative consequences of bad choices. That is *discipling*.

Remember, your objective in this confrontational approach is not just to stop behavior but to use disciplinary encounters as opportunities to *disciple*. If you are genuinely concerned about your students' Spiritual growth, you will guide them in examining their motives.

You can help a student with a guess or two so he/she gets an idea of what you are looking for: "Did someone make fun of you at recess? Did you have a fight with your parents this morning? Did you get cut from the basketball team?"

I am certain you will get one or more of a number of typical responses. If they don't want the class' attention, they will probably say they are sorry. More than likely, they don't really mean it. They just want to either stay out of trouble, or avoid the scrutiny of their peers. They might not even know why you are talking to them. They just want you to move on.

On the other hand, they might say that they don't know why they are doing what they are doing. That may be correct because most students have not been asked to and do not know how to examine their lives enough to understand why they do the things they do. Help them to understand the importance of knowing why we do what we do. Assure them that you don't just want them to stop their behavior, but that you know it will be helpful in the future if they practice recognizing the reasons for their actions. This will take time. It is a skill that takes practice to develop, but it is the fulfilling work of *discipling* we have been called to do.

Another popular response is the question, "Why you are picking on me when everybody else is doing it, too?" Be honest with them. Take a moment to give an answer. They are asking you to tell them why you are doing what you are doing. It is a fair question—teachers are sinners, too. If you can't answer without incriminating yourself, you are probably on the wrong track anyway. I usually respond with a statement about how I am more concerned about them at that moment than the other students—that they need my attention more than the others in this situation.

As the student struggles with thinking about his/her motives, ask the class if they have noticed the behavior and if they have any clues as to why he/she may be acting out. This is the community building part of the process. This is not a time for tattling but for showing true concern for a fellow student. The class should be reminded that if the student being *discipled* has revealed something to them in confidence, that confidentiality should not be broken. Assure them that you are not prying into their private lives but rather looking for clues that might help them understand why they do what they do. We are all painfully aware of HIPPA laws and need to respect our students' privacy. However, I am confident that this process can be used without jeopardizing the breaking of any laws. Our concern for Christian community should not be overcome by a culture that does not value community as Christians do. Almost every situation can be used to teach the other students important life skills. You are not wasting their time. That is why we teach in a Christian school in the first place and, hopefully, why their parents have sent them to our school.

If the student comes up with what sounds like a legitimate reason why he/she is acting out, talk about it. Give the student some under-standing and empathize with his/her situation. If the student can't think of a reason, encourage him/her to keep working on it. The reality is that there is always a reason why we do what we do. It is impossible to act in a vacuum. Even God gives us motives for His actions: "God so loved ...that He gave" (John 3:16). Understanding our motives gives us a fighting chance to get our actions in sync with what God wants for our own good. Remember, our motives are evaluated along with our actions when God judges. "All a man's ways seem innocent to him, but motives are weighed by the Lord" (Prov. 16:2 NIV).

Then, whether it is a good reason or not, help the student begin strategizing what he/she can do in the future to make better choices. Help him/her list some of the better ideas and then choose one or two of them to practice. You may want to write them down and give the student a copy.

Finally, close the sale. Salesmen tell me that the most important step of sealing a deal is to ask for a commitment to the sale. "Will you buy my product?" Surprisingly, it is the step most often overlooked. In *discipling* we need to do the same thing. Ask the student if he/she can commit to a new way of behaving. Jesus said, "Go and sin no more." Ask him/her if he/she understands what you are saying and if he/she can see how it would work better for him/her and everyone else. Then ask him/her if he/she is willing to act accordingly.

You may have noticed in my confrontation with Chris that the step of "closing the sale" was not taken. That was because it was the first day of the school year and I was new to the school. No element of trust had been established yet. Fortunately, Chris did commit to a more acceptable pattern of behavior on his own. I have had many other experiences similar to this one, and because I was not so new to the situation, I spent more time exploring causes for the behavior and helping students understand themselves. Because a base of trust existed, I did more negotiating for the behavior to which the individual was willing to commit.

I assure you that if this confrontational approach is applied in an age appropriate manner, and all the previous chapters are in place, you will see the *discipling* effect it has on all but the most defiant of students. For those who do not respond to your intervention, your principal should have a similar but more consequential process.

Some concern has been voiced that confrontation and bringing other students in on the discussion of another student's problems is not showing respect. However, community building is exactly what is needed, not isolation. St. Paul made that clear when he confronted Peter about his hypocrisy regarding his association with Gentiles: "But when Cephas came to Antioch, I opposed him to his face, because he stood condemned. [12] For before certain men came from James, he was eating with the Gentiles; but when they came he drew back and separated himself, fearing the circumcision party. [13] And the rest of the Jews acted hypocritically along with him, so that even Barnabas was led astray by their hypocrisy. [14] But when I saw that their conduct was not in step with the truth of the gospel, I said to Cephas before them all, 'If you, though a Jew, live like a Gentile and not like a Jew, how can you force the Gentiles to live like Jews?'" (Gal. 2:11-14). If our respect and love for our students is clear and our motive is to benefit the whole community, it will not cause shame or embarrassment.

One of my pet complaints about the disciplinary atmosphere of most schools is that rules are written because teachers and administrators do not have the courage to confront a student that is misbehaving. Instead, they write rules to address the misbehavior of a small percentage of the student body; then all the students must endure the same restrictions. This weakens community and is contrary to *discipling* discipline. If we are not willing to treat our students using the building blocks and confrontational discipline or something similar to it, we really don't believe in the "communion of saints, the forgiveness of sins" as confessed in the third article of the Apostles' Creed.

Another problem I see in classrooms and school systems is that we put our school rules on the same level as sins against the Ten Commandments. I agree that disobedience to a teacher or administrator is a sin; but haven't we elevated our rules to the status of being God-given when we treat them the same as Biblical law? There is also confusion as to what is sin and what is not sin. When we think of "our brother sinning against us" (Matthew 18:15) and misbehavior that is dealt with in the classroom, we must realize these are two different things. Mistakenly, we often use Matthew 18 as a guide for disciplinary procedure in the classroom. We should condemn sins against God, but the breaking of man-made rules are not in the same category. Shouldn't forgetting to wear a belt be dealt with differently than using God's name in vain?

Students will probably be shocked by this approach to their behavior because of the culture in which they live. This process ultimately leads to accountability which is what Jesus was after when he confronted His listeners. Our society no longer holds individuals accountable for their behaviors. This practice seems counterintuitive as we look at the emphasis on individuality we simultaneously hold so dearly as Americans.

Any number of laws and court decisions illustrate our unwillingness to hold the individual accountable while at the same time protecting the individual's freedoms. Both of these concepts are contrary to Scripture. God calls us to confess our sin. This is accountability. He also calls us to a commitment to the well-being of the body of Christ and even our enemies. This is community. If we want to help our students build a bright future, we need to convince them of these principles. I can think of no better time to do that than at moments of mild crises in their lives. Change most often happens when there is an emotional experience associated with an event that is significant enough to make a lasting impression. When used wisely, the process of confrontational discipline creates such an experience.

A word of caution: we are not doctors or family therapists. We cannot deal with pathological conditions or severely dysfunctional situations. At that point, we and our students are best served by a referral to Christian professionals who can handle the situation. You are equipped to be a fellow Christian and a teacher for them, so stick to those roles.

How do we decide what to confront and what to let go? Trust your Christian instincts, your previous experiences, your professionalism, and your love and respect for your students. Pray about it, seek the Holy Spirit's guidance in His Word, and let your desire to serve Him and the students lead you.

QUESTIONS FOR FURTHER DISCUSSION:

1. How can you confront students without embarrassing or humiliating them?

_____

_____

_____

2. Why does Christian confrontation not create animosity between the two parties?

_____

_____

_____

3. How does a student's recognition that his/her actions are a choice help him/her change behavior?

_____

_____

_____

4. What is the difference between "confronting discipline" and punishment?

_____

_____

_____

5. What school-wide rules exist that address problems that only a few students are causing?

_____

_____

_____

6. Why is saying "I'm sorry" not enough to create accountability?

_____

_____

_____

7. Debate: "For a Christian, **everything** is a choice."

_____

_____

_____

8. What changes would you make in the confrontational process for different age levels?

_____

_____

_____

9. How did Jesus confront the woman at the well in John 4:1-42?

_____

10. In what way does this passage not apply to students acting out in the classroom?
"If your brother sins against you, go and tell him his fault, between you and him alone. If he listens to you, you have gained your brother. [16] But if he does not listen, take one or two others along with you, that every charge may be established by the evidence of two or three witnesses. [17] If he refuses to listen to them, tell it to the church. And if he refuses to listen even to the church, let him be to you as a Gentile and a tax collector. [18] Truly, I say to you, whatever you bind on earth shall be bound in heaven, and whatever you loose on earth shall be loosed in heaven. [19] Again I say to you, if two of you agree on earth about anything they ask, it will be done for them by my Father in heaven. [20] For where two or three are gathered in my name, there am I among them." (Matthew 18:15-20)

_____

_____

_____

11. In what way does Matthew 18:15-20 encourage confrontation?

_____

_____

_____

12. Why did St. Paul not use the Matthew 18: 15-20 process when confronting Peter?

_____

_____

_____

13. Share an experience when Matthew 18:15b "you have gained your brother" actually happened.

_____

_____

_____

More of God's Word on the Subject: Colossians 3:12ff, Hebrews 12:3-11, II Corinthians 3:18, Matthew 7:21-27

OTHER EXAMPLES

BRUCE: Successful Community

While I was teaching in Detroit, my uncle came to visit my school. I was in the middle of P.E. class with boys from fifth, sixth, seventh and eighth grades—about 30 of them in all. He wanted a tour of the school so I told Bruce, one of the eighth graders, to lead calisthenics while we looked around. I also asked a colleague, whose office overlooked the room they were in, to keep an eye on them--liability, you know. The students did not know that I had spoken to her. When we got back after ten minutes or so, Bruce had all the boys lined up in order of class, waiting patiently for me to return. After leading the exercises, Bruce had taken it upon himself to organize the group and show my uncle and me respect by being ready for our return. My uncle was very impressed, as was I.

Bruce did not do this out of fear of punishment or in order to gain some special treatment. Because we had established community throughout the year, he and the other students did not see that occasion as an opportunity to get away with something in my absence. Instead, they worked *with* me in showing an outsider, my uncle, what we were all about.

TRISH: Behavior has its reasons

While I was principal and seventh and eighth grade teacher in Saginaw, Michigan, the kindergarten teacher came to my office and said something was wrong with Trish. I asked her to elaborate. Trish had been a gentle, obedient, student, eager to learn and respectful of her teacher. In recent days, however, Trish had begun acting out in negative ways. She was rude, abusive to the other students, and curt with her teacher. When the teacher called Trish's father, he showed up in the middle of class, took Trish into the hallway, removed his belt and proceeded to beat her. He returned her to class amid Trish's tears and informed the teacher that she would not have any more trouble with Trish.

Trish's behavior did not change and for obvious reasons, the teacher did not want to call the father again. I asked the secretary to sit in on my class—liability you know—and took Trish into the library. After some reluctance, she began to talk to me. As it turned out, her parents had taken her to a horror film where monsters came into children's rooms at night and hurt or kidnapped them. Trish was so afraid that the monsters were coming for her that she kept herself awake all night. That way, she reasoned, she could run if she heard or saw the monsters coming.

When I asked why she hadn't told her parents, she said that they would be angry with her. They had told her to not watch the scary parts of the film, but she had peeked through her fingers during those parts in spite of her parents' instruction. I convinced Trish that the movie was make-believe. I assured her that I would talk to her parents about her disobedience at the movie and was sure she would not be punished for it.

This example illustrates that there are reasons for a child's misbehavior. Had we simply changed behavior, we would never have discovered Trish's overwhelming fear. If we had used her father's methods, nothing would have changed, at least not for a long time. As it was, Trish began to sleep again, and her demeanor improved immediately. The teacher's love for her student motivated her to not only make her classroom an easier place to teach, but to also help a struggling child of God.

TED: Use of law and gospel

Ted was bragging to his friends how he had stolen a really neat pen from the local drug store. He was telling them in such a way that I could easily overhear. I could have told him that stealing was a sin, that God would punish him for it, and that he should take it back. Instead, I asked him *why* he would take something that didn't belong to him. He said that if the stores were stupid enough to make it so easy to steal, that he would do just that. I asked if he needed the pen or whether it just the thrill of getting away with something. He wasn't sure. I asked if it bothered him when he prayed to God at night. He said he didn't pray much. I saw this as an opportunity to have a long give and take about his spiritual life. He had never made the connection between what he was learning in religion classes and his daily life. At the end of our discussion, he told me that he had decided to put the pen back, and added that he would like to talk to God more often. I know that Ted grew spiritually that day; he actually desired change in his life because I did not treat him like a loser or beat him over the head with the law.

DISCUSSION TOPICS:

1. Encourage one another by sharing times when the Holy Spirit led you to treat students with loving respect, thereby *discipling* them.

_____

_____

_____

2. Discuss what part of these experiences could have been more Christ-like.

_____

_____

_____

3. Inventory your own stories and examples of confrontational intervention with a law/gospel approach and examples when you did not merely impose rules.

_____

_____

_____

CONCLUSION

I know a loving and caring teacher who has classroom management problems. When I tried to encourage him to use a confrontational approach in order to be more effective in the classroom, he said, "I could never do that. That would make me too uncomfortable." How sad. His own comfort was more important to him than his students' future as *disciples*.

Christian teaching is not about our comfort. It is about the souls of those God has entrusted to our care. It is about using every opportunity possible to equip students for a joyful life in Jesus. God continually calls us to actions that make us uncomfortable. *Discipling* is our calling. It is one of the opportunities to serve Him that can, at times, move us out of our comfort zone and challenge us to take risks in order to fulfill our mission. Ultimately, the next generation of committed *disciples* will be empowered to do His work, in part, by how we discipline and *disciple*.

I pray that a significant portion of what has been presented is "preaching to the choir" and will serve to reinforce what you already believe to be true and are currently practicing. I also pray that I have introduced ideas that may not have occurred to you—ideas that challenge the status quo of your disciplining/*discipling* process. If so, I ask the Holy Spirit to lead you to incorporate them into the carrying out of your Mission and Ministry as a Christian teacher.

APPENDIX A

CONSEQUENCES *plus* GRACE

1. I'm sorry and I promise it won't happen again. Because I really am sorry and it won't happen again, that should excuse me from the consequences of my behavior.

2. I'm sorry. I understand that I have to suffer the consequences of my choices and conduct. I'll take my punishment, pay my pound of flesh, and balance the scales of justice by paying for my sin.

3. I may or may not be sorry. I'm willing to take the consequences of my decisions. I've thought through the implications and have weighed the possible outcomes. The decision is worth the cost.

4. I now understand that my decisions and actions are always shaded by sin that I both can and cannot

anticipate. This complex reality does not excuse me from a life of decisions. I must live and act since "not to decide *is* to decide." And I understand about consequences. But I also understand that consequences, good or bad, cannot ultimately justify my decisions since even good ones are always tainted by sin—that sometimes you cannot un-ring a bell. Therefore, I will live and act not only according to consequences but also under the canopy of God's grace—grace that will ultimately triumph over all temporal consequences.

LUTHER ON RANK AND SUPERIORITY

Among Christians there shall and can be no authority; but all are alike subject to one another, as Paul says in Rom. 12:10, "Each shall count the other his superior," and Peter in I Peter 5:5, "All of you be subject to one another." This is also what Christ means in Luke 14:10, "When you are invited to a marriage, go and sit in the lowest place."

There is no superior among Christians except Christ himself and Christ alone. And what kind of authority can there be when all are equal and have the same right, power, possession, and honor, and no one desires to be the other's superior, but each the other's inferior?

One could not establish authority where there are such people, even if one would, since their character and nature will not permit them to have superiors, for no one is willing or able to be the superior. But where there are no such people, there are no real Christians. What are the priests and bishops then? I answer: Their government is not one of authority or power, but a service and an office, for they are neither higher nor better than other Christians.

"Treatise on Secular Authority: To What Extent It Should Be Obeyed."

WHOM DO YOU THINK YOU'RE TALKING TO?

How shall we helpfully and evangelically
address different people in their various
Spiritual conditions?

	Alarmed by Their Sin	Secure in Their Sin
Within the Household of God	GOSPEL	LAW
Outside the Household of God	GOSPEL	Depends: see I Cor. 5 esp. v.12 Jonah 3:1-10 Luke 9:51-56 Acts 17:16-34*

*Modes of engagement for those outside the
household of faith: witness, dialog, apologetics,
exploration, representation, ambassadorship,
invitation, introduction to Jesus. Engagement is
guided by Biblically informed judgment.

APPENDIX D

References: Jesus asks "WHY?"

Matthew	Mark	Luke	John
6:28	2:8	2:49	2:4
8:26	4:40	5:22	7:19
9:4	5:39	6:41	7:23
14:31	8:12	6:46	8:43
15:3	8:17	12:26	8:46
16:8	10:18	12:57	10:36
19:17	12:16	18:19	18:23
20:6	14:6	22:46	
22:18		24:38	
26:10			

CPSIA information can be obtained at www.ICGtesting.com
Printed in the USA
BVOW07s1825240713

326879BV00001B/6/P